How to Buy Gold

How to Buy Gold

by Timothy Green

Walker and Company . New York

First published in the United States of America in 1975 by the Walker Publishing Company, Inc.

Published simultaneously in Canada by Fitzhenry & Whiteside, Limited, Toronto.

ISBN: 0-8027-0478-6 (cloth)

ISBN: 0-8027-7095-9 (paper)

Library of Congress Catalog Card Number: 74-29119

Printed in the United States of America.

Designed by Barbara Bedick

10 9 8 7 6 5 4 3 2 1

Contents

Preface

This short book, *How to Buy Gold*, is intended as a swift guide to the ordinary American who is now able to hoard gold privately for the first time in a generation. It really complements two earlier books of mine, *The World of Gold* and *The World of Gold Today*, which describe in detail who mines, who markets, who buys, and who smuggles gold.

I would like to give special thanks to Beth Walker, wife of my New York publisher, who really triggered off the book by asking "if I have $5,000 how do I go out and buy gold, and what exactly do I get?" And to her husband, Sam Walker, who promptly suggested I should do a book to answer that for all Americans.

I am grateful to a number of leading American bullion dealers and banks who were good enough to provide me with advance information of their gold marketing plans. My two assistants, Sue Weait and Fionnuola Flood, also did a noble job helping me pull together a mass of information in a matter of weeks.

But any misinterpretations and errors are entirely of my own making. Moreover, with a wildly fluctuating gold price, the prices quoted here are subject to change. But judging how the price may jump is, of course, half the art of buying gold.

T.S.G.
Dulwich, November, 1974.

How to Buy Gold

1 *The Golden Opportunity*

For the first time in most people's memory, the American citizen is free to buy gold. Ever since 1933, when President Franklin D. Roosevelt issued a Presidential Order banning the private buying of gold within the United States, gold holding has been limited to a few gold coins.

Suddenly, however, gold is going to be all around you. It will gleam seductively from the windows and counters of coin dealers, department stores, and spe-

cialty shops. Advertisements in the newspapers, magazines, and on television will try to woo you into buying
it. "More men have been knocked off balance by gold
than by love," Benjamin Disraeli once told the British
House of Commons. Will Americans now have a love
affair with gold?

If you want to fall for gold, how should you go about
it? Should you buy some exotic piece of gold jewelery,
or perhaps a handy little bar no bigger than a luscious
gold-coated chocolate, or like some Spanish pirate, settle for golden pieces of eight or equally exotic coins?
This book sets out to tell you how, why, where, and
when you should buy gold; it is a guide to the language
and the mysteries of the world of gold.

Although John Maynard Keynes once called gold a
"barbarous relic," it still clings tenaciously to men's
hearts. The importance that bankers still attach to gold
as an essential bastion of a nation's wealth is more than
equaled by ordinary people the world over who still see
gold as a sheet anchor against devaluations, insecure
currencies, and the hazards of war. The French, re-
membering two invasions of their country in a generation, still like to keep a little store of gold; the Italians
now faced with a debt-ridden economy and political
unrest have been buying gold coins; and even the Ca-
nadians queued up at bank counters in recent months
to get a piece of the action as the gold price soared.

Gold is now making a comeback after lying low for
years. With the price fixed at $35 an ounce back in

1934 and remaining at that level until 1968, it was hardly an attractive investment. Today, however, gold has broken right away from that price straitjacket and is zooming up and away, like some liberated honeybee, delighted to be free and not sure where to settle. Anyone who was smart enough to get aboard at the beginning of the ride has done very handsomely. After all, as the Dow Jones index came tumbling down, the gold price went rocketing up.

So far, Americans have had to watch the fun from the sidelines (unless they bought illegally in Canada or through intermediaries in Switzerland), but from December 31, 1974, they have been able to climb aboard. The whole dazzling range of gold bars and coins is there for the taking (if you can afford them).

Gold jewelery, of course, has been on sale all the time, but we should be quite clear at the outset that gold bullion and coin are quite distinct from jewelery. Most of the jewelery you can buy is only 10 or 14 carat; it is not pure gold. Pure gold is 24 carat and is too soft to be made up into normal jewelery. More important, the gold jewelery you can buy has a markup of anything between 100% and 200% over the actual gold content. So if you buy a 14 carat ring weighing 0.25 ounce, it will actually contain only 0.15 ounce of pure gold. At current gold prices (around $180 an ounce), that 0.15 ounce is worth about $27, but you will pay at least $60-$70 (probably more) for the ring. And if you try to resell it, you may only get the value of the metal

in it. So gold jewelery cannot be looked on as an investment, unless it is a real antique (and thus has rarity
value), or unless the gold price doubles or triples.

The action, therefore, is in gold bars and coins that
are nearly pure gold. Just to complicate matters, their
purity is not judged in carats, but in fineness. Completely pure gold is 1,000 fine; that is to say one thousand parts per thousand pure gold. And any gold bars
that are 995 fine (i.e., 995 parts per 1,000 gold) are
classed as bullion. Gold coins are usually 900 or 916.6
fine, although a few, like the Austrian 4 ducat, are
986.6 fine.

Gold, like other precious metals, is weighed either in
troy ounces (1 troy ounce = 1.1 ounces avoirdupois), or
on the metric scale in grams and kilos. In the United
States gold weights will usually be in troy ounces, but
kilo bars (32.15 ounces) and ½ kilo bars will also be on
sale.

Although gold remains as one of the anchor points of
our international monetary system and is still the only
universally accepted medium by which one nation,
whether capitalist or communist, can settle its debts
with another, a curious divorce has taken place since
1968 between gold's official monetary role and its place
in the private sector. Up to 1968 there was one basic
price for gold ($35 an ounce) on which all monetary
and non-monetary (i.e., for jewelery or private investment) purchases were based. But in that year the two-
tier market for gold was created; under this, monetary

GOLD PURITY

Jewelry		Bars and Coins
24 carats	=	1000 fine
22 carats	=	916.66 fine
20 carats	=	833.33 fine
18 carats	=	750 fine
14 carats	=	583.33 fine
10 carats	=	416.66 fine

GOLD WEIGHTS

Troy		Metric and Grains
1 troy ounce	=	31. 1035 grams
1 troy ounce	=	480 grains
1 troy ounce	=	20 pennyweight
32.15 troy ounces	=	1 kilogram
32150 troy ounces	=	1 metric tonne

gold was still set at $35 an ounce, while the price in the so-called "free" market for non-monetary purchases was allowed to float. That free market price has now floated on up to over $180 an ounce. The official monetary price, at which governments should exchange gold to settle international payments, still lags far behind. It is now $42.22, following the two devaluations of the dollar.

In practice, of course, governments are simply refusing to exchange gold with each other at $42.22. They are sitting on their gold reserves and, in their unofficial books, revaluing them at the current free market price, while making international settlements in currencies or Special Drawing Rights. The myth that official monetary gold is still valued at $42.22 was blown when Italy used her gold, valued at $120 an ounce, as collateral for a loan from Germany in 1974.

But in the meantime, the two-tier price remains as a formality. The gold you buy will be priced at the free market rate.

2 Why Buy Gold?

Gold does not pay interest or dividends, so why buy it anyway? There are two prime reasons.

First, to make money.

Second, to avoid losing money. And in an age of inflation and currency devaluations, the second reason may be almost a better one than the first. Gold at least holds its value as paper money declines.

But to begin with, let's look at gold's money-making track record. After years in which its performance was nil—that is to say, it stayed at $35 an ounce from 1934 through to 1968—it has suddenly begun to pay off handsomely in the 1970's. Anyone who was smart enough to buy gold in 1970 has already been able to reap a 500% profit. The price, as late as December 1970, was still hovering around $35 an ounce; by April 3, 1974 (the day after President Pompidou of France died), it had hit $179.50. True, it then dropped back to around $130 in the summer of 1974, but it was coming on strongly again at well over $180 in November 1974. So anyone who got onto the bandwagon rather late in, say, July 1974, could still have notched up a 20% profit just four months later.

Some gold coins, including those like the $20 double eagle that Americans were already allowed to hold before complete liberalization, have done even better. The bonus with gold coins can be the premium they command over their gold content. This premium fluctuates according to the rarity of the coin and current demand, but even on regularly minted gold coins like the Austrian crowns, Mexican pesos, and the South African Krugerrand the variation can be enough to pay extra dividends to the buyer who purchases at the right moment. The premiums on the Mexican and Austrian coins, for instance, fluctuated from as low as 5% to up to 18% over their gold content in 1974, while the premium on the U.S. $20 double eagle, which was around 40% a few years ago, shot up to 86% in 1974. If you were astute enough to buy a double eagle in 1967 it cost only $48, but in late 1974 was worth $300.

So gold can turn in a handsome profit. But anyone buying gold in 1975 should realize that it is unlikely to jump another 500% in the next four years, thus repeating what it has done in the last four. What has really been happening since 1970 is that the gold price has been making up lost ground for all those years from 1934 when it was officially pegged at $35. The price of all other precious metals had soared during the period that gold had been kept artificially fixed. So gold had a lot of catching up to do.

But if another 500% bonus is not immediately in prospect, there is good money to be made by the shrewd investor who takes advantage of the wide fluctuations of the gold price. After years in which the price hardly moved a cent or two, a shift up (or down) of $5-$10 a day has become quite commonplace.

Just look at what happened in 1974. The year began with the price at $114.75 an ounce, but it was up to $141 by the end of January; in the next three months it soared onward to a high of $179.50 in April, then came back to $154 in May and down to $129 on July 4, before rallying on up to $185 in early November. The increased U.S. demand in 1975 may well push it up to $200 and beyond. Some gold bugs are even talking of gold at $300. Even if that is speculative, there is no doubt that anyone who played the gold market game well in 1974 came out ahead of most people caught in Wall Street's decline.

LONDON GOLD PRICES

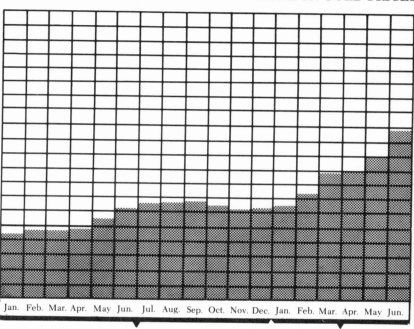

Jan. Feb. Mar. Apr. May Jun. Jul. Aug. Sep. Oct. Nov. Dec. Jan. Feb. Mar. Apr. May Jun.

1972   1973

JANUARY 1972 TO NOVEMBER 1974°   DOLLARS PER OUNCE

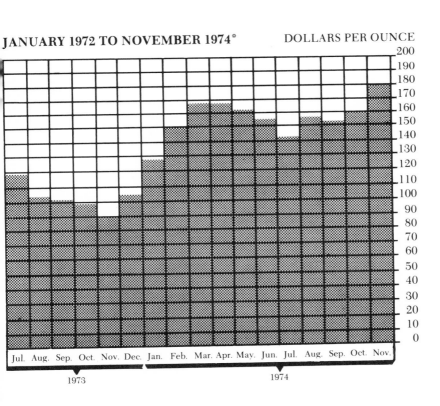

°Figures are derived from a monthly average of prices.

But the reason for buying gold is not simply to make money. It is also an excellent hedge against losing it. While gold cannot always keep you ahead of inflation, it can protect you from currency devaluations. Remember that the dollar has been devalued twice recently, in December 1971 and in February 1973. On both occasions anyone holding gold came out all square, as the monetary price changed first from $35 to $38 and then to the present official price of $42.22 an ounce. And since the U.S. is still faced with continuing balance of payments deficits, as oil prices soar, so gold remains a hedge against any further devaluations.

Gold's value as a hedge against insecure currencies has long been part of its appeal to many people in Europe, especially the French who have faced some sixteen devaluations of their currency since 1914. As the French franc has repeatedly become worth less against other currencies, so the Frenchmen have learnt that by keeping part of their savings in gold they at least do not lose on successive devaluations. For Americans long regarding the dollar to be "as good as gold," such hedging did not seem necessary until the last few years. But the two devaluations of the dollar have been harsh reminders that paper money can become worth less (if not worthless) overnight.

And if you are thinking of buying gold, it is worth keeping a couple of other points in mind. After all, what makes gold the noblest of metals? Its great strength is its indestructability. Unlike silver it does not tarnish, and it is corroded only by a special mix of nitric and hydrochloric acid. Gold coins have been recovered from sunken treasure ships after two centuries beneath the sea, looking as bright as new. Gold, like diamonds, is forever.

An additional reason for buying gold is, quite simply, that it remains today the only universally accepted medium of exchange; the ultimate way in which one country, whether capitalist or communist, settles its debts with another. Although Lenin once suggested that when a true socialist society had been achieved gold would be used only to cover the walls and floors of public lavatories, he conceded that until such a day the Soviet Union must carefully save its gold. "Sell it at the highest price, buy goods with it at the lowest price," he recommended. Adding, "When living among wolves, howl like the wolves."

Well, in the dangerous days in which we now live, it may not hurt to join the wolves. I always remember the old London gold dealer who first told me much of what I know about the metal remarking that "gold is bedrock." And in the 1970's it is good to have your feet very firmly on the ground.

That fine playwright George Bernard Shaw had it all worked out, of course. His widely quoted advice on gold was unequivocal. In the *Intelligent Woman's Guide to Socialism and Capitalism* he wrote, "You have to choose [as a voter], between trusting to the natural stability of gold and the honesty and intelligence of members of the government. And, with due respect for these gentlemen, I advise you, as long as the capitalist system lasts, to vote for gold."

3 Where the Gold Comes From

The United States itself is the world's fourth largest producer of gold, with output now running at around 35 tons annually, worth over $200 million at a gold price of $150 an ounce. Three-quarters of all this gold comes from just four main producers: Homestake Mining Co., at Lead, South Dakota; Kennecott Copper Corporation, who win gold as a by-product of their giant open-cast copper mine at Bingham Canyon in Utah; Carlin Gold Mining Co. at Eureka, Nevada; and Cortez Gold Mines at Lander, Nevada. These produc-

ers sell their gold either directly to jewelery manufacturers as part of long-term contracts, or market it
through leading bullion dealers like Engelhard and
Handy and Harman.

But for many years U.S. domestic production has not
been enough to satisfy even the basic demands of jewelery and industry in the nation, which call for over 200
tons a year. Substantial imports of gold have therefore
been necessary and these will be even more essential
once private gold holding is permitted—unless the
Treasury decides to sell gold on the free market direct
from the U.S. official monetary reserves.

The closest source of gold is Canada, the world's
third largest producer, where mining yields about 60
tons of gold a year. Most of this gold is marketed
through two major outlets, the Noranda Sales Corporation and the Bank of Nova Scotia, both in Toronto. In
recent years these outlets have been selling most of
Canada's surplus gold, after deducting requirements
for her own jewelery industry and private hoarding, directly onto the market in New York. In 1973, for instance, Canadian gold exports to the U.S. were over 40
tons.

Even this, however, is not enough to cater to all
requirements, and the U.S. is dependent on large imports of gold from the world's two gold-mining giants,
South Africa and Russia.

For more than a decade South Africa has produced
over 75% of all the gold in the non-communist world,
and well over a half of all gold mined, including Rus-

sian production. In 1973 South Africa mined 852.3 tons of gold out of total estimated world production of 1,499 tons. In 1974 her production was down to around 770 tons, because the higher gold price was enabling much lower grade ore to be mined, but she remains the un-challenged leader. (See Table 1 below.)

TABLE 1
GOLD PRODUCTION 1968-1974

	1968	1969	1970	1971	1972	1973	1974°
South Africa	969.4	972.8	1000.0	976.6	908.7	852.3	770
U.S.S.R	304.2	318.2	335.5	344.8	360.2	370.6	390
Canada	83.6	79.2	74.9	68.7	64.7	60.0	55
U.S.A.	46.0	53.9	54.2	46.4	45.1	36.5	36.3
Other Africa	47.1	45.8	44.4	44.6	42.3	44.8	48
Latin America	33.5	35.5	35.4	34.1	34.9	36.0	36.0
Asia	30.0	31.8	33.1	33.2	33.5	34.5	34.00
Europe	6.7	6.9	7.4	7.6	13.2	14.3	15.0
Australia	24.3	22.2	19.5	20.9	23.5	18.4	16.1
Papua/New Guinea	0.8	0.8	0.7	0.7	12.7	20.3	19.0
Communist Countries	8.4	8.4	8.4	8.4	8.4	8.4	8.4
Other	3.6	3.2	3.6	3.1	3.2	3.2	3.2
TOTAL WORLD PRODUCTION	1557.6	1578.7	1617.1	1589.1	1550.4	1499.3	1431

Source: Consolidated Gold Fields, London.
° 1974 estimates by author.

The Russians have kept the precise figures of their production secret for a generation, but the latest estimates (by the London mining finance firm Consolidated Gold Fields) set Soviet output at 370.6 tons in 1973 and 390 tons for 1974. Part of this gold is used for industry within the Soviet Union, but in recent years a major slice has also been sold in the West, to earn vital foreign exchange required for wheat and other imports. In 1973 Russian sales of gold totaled about 280 tons and were projected at 200 tons for 1974.

Both the South Africans and the Russians have been selling their gold through the world's two great wholesale markets, Zurich and London. Up to 1968 all South African gold went via the London market, but since then, 80% of it has been marketed through a consortium of the three leading Swiss Banks: Swiss Bank Corporation, Swiss Credit Bank, and Union Bank of Switzerland in Zurich. The Russians have sold their gold to these banks and selected London dealers via their own Wozchod Bank in Zurich.

However, with the opening up of the U.S. market in 1975, leading American dealers are hoping to persuade both the South Africans and perhaps even the Russians to sell directly to them. Even without direct sales, U.S. dealers will be major customers for South African and Russian gold on the two European markets. Moreover, the three Swiss banks, and the five members of the London gold market (Johnson Matthey, Mocatta and Goldsmid, Samuel Montagu, N.M. Rothschild, and

Sharps Pixley) will all be working closely with leading U.S. dealers to facilitate supplies. Mocatta and Goldsmid already has its own direct linkup in the U.S., with the Mocatta Metals Corporation in New York; Samuel Montagu made a tieup in October 1974 with Handy and Harman (leading U.S. bullion dealers) and Merrill Lynch for a joint gold-marketing operation in the U.S.; while Sharps Pixley has had its own New York office for some years.

So even if the South Africans and Russians choose to continue selling exclusively to Zurich and London, the bullion men there are already over the threshold in the United States.

The alternative source of gold for American buyers is the U.S.'s own monetary stocks of gold, which the Treasury has indicated it may also sell on the free market. These stocks stood at just over 8,500 tons late in 1974; that is equivalent to about six years' demand in the private, non-monetary sector worldwide. A major slice of these stocks (nearly 5,000 tons) are held at Fort Knox in Kentucky; the rest is in U.S. government vaults in New York, San Francisco, Denver, and Philadelphia. The U.S. Treasury may well decide to sell some of this gold to private American buyers in 1975, both to prevent too large a drain on the balance of payments through gold imports and to push the gold price down if American private demand sends it soaring. The Treasury would undoubtedly like to point out to U.S. citizens that it is possible to lose money by holding gold, as well as making it, so they might wait until the price soared spectacularly and then try to flood the market.

If the Treasury does sell, they are expected to market their gold through the General Services Administration, which has already sold other metals like silver for the U.S. government over the years. The GSA will probably "auction" the gold, by announcing that x ounces are available for tender, and inviting sealed bids for any quantity up to that maximum at any price. Bullion dealers would then put in their bids (if they chose to compete), and the GSA would reserve the right to accept or reject any tenders submitted.

The real issue here is how much of its monetary stocks of gold the U.S. is prepared to lay on the line to be snapped up by the private U.S. gold investor. Clearly the U.S. cannot afford to put all its 8,500 tons at risk; it must keep a strategic stock. Moreover, U.S. official gold stocks have been seriously depleted already over the last twenty years; in 1949 the U.S. proudly held three-quarters of the world's monetary stocks of gold. But during the 1960's the continuing U.S. balance-of-payments deficits led to an outflow of gold to Western Europe, where such countries as West Germany, France, Italy, and the Netherlands built up their reserves by trading in surplus dollars to the U.S. for gold. President Nixon stopped that in August 1971 when he announced that dollars were no longer convertible into gold, but by that time the U.S. had only 8,500 tons of the world's monetary stock of 37,000 tons of gold. The

U.S. is unlikely now to hand out all the rest to its private citizens.

Nor is much of that total monetary stock of 37,000 tons likely to come onto the private market. In these days of inflation and soaring oil prices, Western nations with large gold reserves prefer to sit on them and watch them appreciate as the free market price of gold rises. It is the one great asset they hold; the trump card—as the Italians found in 1974 when they were able to pledge part of their gold reserves to West Germany in return for a crucial loan to enable them to meet oil payments.

So it is unlikely that much of this mountain of monetary gold will be made available to the private U.S. gold buyer. Most of the gold he buys will have to come from new mine production, which now runs at about 1,350-1,400 tons a year. And this production is actually declining as mining companies are able to dig out more low-grade ore at present high prices; this lengthens the life of a mine, but reduces output on an annual basis. The supply of new gold is shrinking by about 50 tons a year.

Since existing supplies were already being absorbed readily by jewelery and industry (about 500 tons in 1974), gold coins (260 tons), and private investors in Europe, South America, and the Middle East, the added American private demand in 1975 can well push up the gold price considerably. (See Table 2.)

So what price should you pay for gold? That is the topic of the next chapter.

TABLE 2
WHERE GOLD HAS BEEN GOING

Supplies to free market:	1973	1974°
Non-communist world output	1120 tons	1032 tons
Russian sales	280	200
Central bank sales	6	not available
	1406 tons	2132 tons
Offtake:		
Jewelry and industry	794.4 tons	500 tons
Official gold coins	53.2	260
Investors/speculators	558.4	472
	1406 tons	1232 tons

Source 1973 figures: Consolidated Gold Fields, London.
° All 1974 figures are provisional estimates by author.

TABLE 3
OFFICIAL GOLD HOLDINGS*

	30, June 1973	End 1972	End 1968	End 1963
U.S.A.	11,652	10,487	10,892	15,596
Canada	927	834	863	817
Belgium	1,1781	1,638	1,524	1,371
France	4,268	3,826	3,877	3,175
Italy	3,483	3,130	2,923	2,343
Netherlands	2,292	2,059	1,697	1,601
Portugal	1,136	1,021	856	497
Switzerland	3,513	3,158	2,624	2,820
United Kingdom	900	800	1,474	2,484
Western Germany	4,958	4,459	4,539	3,843
Other Western Europe	2,283	2,052	2,268	1,700
Republic of South Africa	804	681	1,243	630
Other Africa	485	440	380	90
Japan	891	801	356	289
Other Asia	765	720	755	625
Latin America	1,250	1,130	1,035	1,170
Middle East	1,200	1,075	1,090	790
Rest of World	566	501	540	379
International Organisations (IMF etc.)	6,751	6,093	1,969	2,080
	49,905	44,905	40,905	42,300

* In millions of dollars, at $35 per fine ounce until 1971; at $38 in 1972; at $42.22 in 1973.

Source: International Monetary Fund.

4 *How to Get the Best Price*

The international price of gold is set twice a day in London, at a ceremony called the "fixing," which dates back to 1919. The five members of the London gold market all meet at Rothschild's, that aristocrat of merchant banking houses, at precisely 10:30 A.M. and at 3 P.M. to "fix" the price, based on their current buying and selling orders. The London price is accepted worldwide as the basic guide for the day. The second London fixing, at 3 P.M. (10 A.M. New York time), usually sets the American price for the day, as it coincides with the opening of the markets in North America. The price is fixed in U.S. dollars per troy ounce (31.1035 grams).

Since 1968, two leading U.S. bullion dealers, Engelhard Minerals & Chemicals Corporation and Handy and Harman have also quoted daily prices, which are usually between 25 cents and 50 cents an ounce higher than London (reflecting the fact that much of the gold for the U.S. market has to be imported, so insurance and freight costs are involved).

Both the London and American domestic quotes are published in the newspapers daily, and you will also find them carried by Reuter's Money Monitor System and the wire services. From January 1, 1975, other leading American dealers, like Mocatta Metals Corporation, will also be quoting daily prices on the Reuter's Money Monitor System.

Leading bullion firms will be providing banks and other dealers, who are taking their gold, with regular prices throughout the day. These prices may change considerably from hour to hour, but if you go to any local bank that is offering gold they will be able to quote you the latest price.

The actual price you pay will depend very much on how much gold you are buying and in what form. (See Chapters 6 and 7 for precise details of coins and bar sizes available.)

If you go in to buy a small quantity of one to ten

ounces, the bank or dealer will almost certainly quote you a "fixed price of the day" that he will have been given by the bullion wholesale firm with whom he deals. This price will be given to him on the phone or telex first thing each morning, and will hold until the bank closes for the day.

But for larger quantities of gold, certainly for amounts of one kilo (32.15 ounces troy) or more, the bank will be getting variable prices during the day, according to market fluctuations. Policy will naturally vary from bullion dealer to bullion dealer. One leading bullion firm will be requiring the local bank to phone their gold trader for special prices on all sales of 50 ounces or more, but will let the bank sell at a fixed price for the day any quantity less than that.

One thing is certain, the larger your order, the more favorable price you will be quoted and the more it will pay you to shop around. This is particularly true if you want to purchase several hundred ounces (an investment of perhaps $20,000 to $50,000) at one time. Then you should try to get several quotes by going to two or three local banks or gold dealers and asking them to get you the current price. Since the price can change from hour to hour, you should check with two or three suppliers in rapid succession to see who is offering the most favorable terms.

Remember, however, that any price quoted to you will usually be slightly above the current London or New York price, because of freight, insurance, and car-

rying charges to your locality. The basic price also relates to gold that is 995 fine. There is an additional
markup on gold of greater fineness, because a special
(and costly) electrolytic process is involved in purifying
it. Most of the small bars on sale in the U.S. will be
999.5 fine, but on larger bars of 10 ounces, one kilo,
and 100 ounces there will usually be a choice of either
995 or 999.9 bars and also 999.5 on the 100 ounces.

So the price you ultimately pay will depend very
much on both the quantity and quality of gold you
buy. A bar of 995 fine will cost you less than a bar of
999.9 of the same weight.

Let's look at some examples:

a) If you buy the small wafer bars of gold weighing only ½, 1, or 2 ounces, you must be prepared to
be quoted a fixed price of the day that will include a
considerable premium over the gold content. You
will be charged at least 5% premium and perhaps 8%
or more for these bars. That is to say, if the gold
price is $200 an ounce, you would pay at least $210
and probably closer to $220 for a one-ounce bar.

The reason is that these small bars are costly to
make, and involve the bank in just as much paperwork to sell them as do the 100-ounce bars.

b) On the kilo bar (which is most popular with
gold hoarders in Europe, South America, and Asia),
containing 32.15 ounces of gold, you may expect a
premium of at least $1 an ounce and probably up to

$3 an ounce. So with gold at $200 an ounce, the basic gold in a kilo bar would cost $6,430, but it would most likely cost you anything between $6,465 and $6,560.

c) The largest gold bar is the 400-ounce "good delivery" bar, which is the one traded between countries. The gold price of the day in fact relates to the price of these bars at 995 fine. So if you can afford one (and it will cost you $80,000 with gold at $200) this is the cheapest way to buy. You will have only to pay the freight and insurance charges if you actually want it delivered, plus perhaps a nominal handling charge. In fact, for this value it would be much wiser to leave it with your bank or even have it held for your account by a New York dealer.

The premium over the gold content also applies on gold coins. Here the premium varies widely from coin to coin. On the U.S. $20 double eagle it has been over 85% in 1974, while on the regularly produced coins like the South African Krugerrand, the Mexican pesos, the Austrian 100 crowns, and the Hungarian 100 crowns, it can go as low as 5% but will usually be between 8% and 15%.

As with the gold bars, the prices can change from hour to hour, but most coin dealers or banks will simply quote you a fixed price for the day. Again, the price will become more favorable the more coins you buy. Dealers will usually give some kind of discount (perhaps $1 or more per coin) for orders of ten coins or more.

On coins it really pays to shop around, as prices can vary by two or three dollars per coin from dealer to dealer. You can get a good idea of dealers giving the best buys by watching the regular advertisements for gold coins in the business section of *The New York Times*, in the *Wall Street Journal*, or in leading newspapers in the major cities across the nation. But remember that the price quoted in the newspaper ads is inevitably slightly out of date, and should be used only as a guide. If you are actually buying coins, go into a coin shop (or shops) and get the current prices.

One word of caution. You will see some newspaper advertisements offering coins (and even small bars) to be sent by mail. While they may be offered by entirely reputable dealers, remember that the price could have changed since the ad was placed and the coins might now be cheaper than the quoted price. Such offers will usually also include some markup for mailing costs and insurance, so again you may be paying a shade more.

Ideally, go personally to two or three local dealers, compare their prices, and also be sure to ask how much discount they offer on orders of ten coins or more.

Finally, what about *state sales taxes*? As the law now stands you will be liable to state sales taxes if you buy either gold coins or gold bars over the counter in any state except Delaware or New Hampshire. But sales tax does *not* have to be paid if you can show you live out of the state and the gold is mailed to you. It is, of course, also possible to arrange for the gold to be delivered free of tax in Delaware or New Hampshire.

Lobbying is under way to arrange for gold bars (but not gold coins) to be exempt from sales tax, so you should check with your local bank or coin dealer on the precise regulations in your own state. They will certainly be able to advise you if it is at all possible to avoid sales tax in your locality.

Just to recap; when buying gold remember these points:

The more you buy and the larger the bars you buy, the lower the "premium," or markup over gold content.

Shop around for competitive prices, especially if you are buying gold coins.

Remember the gold price fluctuates considerably from day to day, and be sure that the price you are being quoted is up to the minute.

5 *Where to Buy*

Small gold bars, all neatly packaged in sealed plastic bags, may be on sale at your local specialty shops or at downtown department stores. And if you are seeking simply a little (though still not cheap) souvenir to give a nephew or grandchild you may look no farther. The serious gold outlets, however, will be banks, brokerage houses, and coin dealers, plus the major bullion dealers themselves. But the big bullion firms will really be act-ing only as wholesalers and will not normally be inter-

ested in individual accounts, unless you wish to purchase at least $30,000 of gold at a time.

The prime outlets for gold will be banks. Several
hundred of America's 14,000 banks have made arrangements to carry stocks and distribute gold on behalf of
the major bullion dealers. In most instances the banks
will hold "consignment stocks" from the dealers and
will sell the gold on their behalf. Bullion dealers are offering "consignment units," usually valued at around
$25,000 each. A bank can decide how many of these
units to hold, according to the size of deposits and the
number of branches. While it is unlikely that gold will
be gleaming beside the tellers in every small-town
bank, you can expect major banks in the larger towns
to be holding at least a modest stock of gold. However,
because of the security problems in storing gold, you
should not expect every neighborhood branch of even
major banks to be holding gold. The gold will be held
in main offices, and your local branch will relay your
order.

The network of bank outlets in major cities will be
good. In New York, for instance, Republic National
Bank (themselves leading bullion dealers of long standing) will be offering gold retail at all their 18 branches
in the metropolitan area. And First National City Bank
is busy installing a special vault in New York to hold
$1 billion of its clients' gold. In Chicago, the First Na-
tional Bank of Chicago has announced its intention to
sell gold; in Pennsylvania, Girard Trust Bank will be

gold sellers. Down South, Bank of Virginia in Richmond, and First American National Bank of Nashville in Nashville have joined the gold rush. In California, Wells Fargo Bank will be living up to their image of gold-rush days by getting back in the business. (A more detailed list of banks is in the Gold Buyer's Address Book at the end of this book.)

Other outlets are also being developed. In New York, Terminal Trading Company, the check-cashing concern, will be selling gold at its ten branches. Merrill Lynch, Pierce, Fenner & Smith will be marketing gold through all their 262 offices in the United States, as will the stockbrokers Shearson Hayden Stone. Other brokerage firms will follow.

Even jewelers are expected to get into the game. Dealers report early interest from jewelery stores, who plan to sell small gold bars alongside wedding rings and diamond tiaras.

For gold coins there is already an extensive network of dealers and coin shops in every state of the Union (see a selected list in the Gold Buyer's Address Book). These shops, of course, offer not only the more popular gold coins like the Mexican pesos or the Krugerrand, but rare coins as well. Banks will also be offering some, if not all, the regular gold coins listed in Chapter 6. Some coin dealers will also be selling small gold bars, but not all are willing to carry bars, because of the problems of detecting potential fakes in buying back bars. One leading New York coin dealer told me he was reluctant to handle gold bars, because he would need to set up special arrangements for assaying bars he bought back. With gold coins, however, he trusted his own skill, after years of experience, to detect fake coins.

Besides these regular outlets you will see all kinds of gold bars, coins, and medallions advertised in newspapers and magazines. This may be a convenient way to buy for people living in small towns without a coin dealer or local bank handling gold. But you should be careful to check that the advertisement is from a legitimate company before sending a check off into the blue.

Once the gold-buying network is fully sorted out you will always be able to check your Yellow Pages for the names of local gold bar or coin dealers. But in the meantime, your own bank or broker will certainly be able to direct you to the nearest dealer, and even if they are not handling gold themselves, they may be able to arrange the purchase for you.

6 Gold Coins-Ten Best Buys

Americans have been permitted to buy and hold gold coins made prior to 1933 for many years and, since January 1974,have been able to hold gold coins made either prior to 1960 or official government "restrikes" that are currently made but bear old dates. But with the liberalization of gold holding, several new coins can be purchased. Moreover, gold coins will be much more widely available through banks and retail stores.

This chapter looks at the most popular and widely

circulated of the gold coins now available. It is not concerned with rare coins that have special value to numismatists, but rather those that the ordinary investor may wish to buy and sell. The advantage of these coins is that they can be traded readily, and you will find that it is much easier to sell back gold coins to recognized coin dealers rather than to trade in small gold bars (see Chapter 7) to banks.

Gold coin prices do fluctuate from day to day, and the price may also vary from dealer to dealer. Usually there is a spread of 2% to 4% between the bid and the asking price. You will find the prices of all the coins listed below quoted daily in the major newspapers, but you should always ascertain the current day's price when actually buying. You should also seek out the price at two or three coin dealers (a select list is given in the Gold Buyer's Address Book at the end of this book), as it can vary by three or four dollars per coin from shop to shop. Dealers will give a slightly better price if you buy ten or more coins at a time. The discount is often $1 or more per coin. For a really large purchase you can also ask for central bank-sealed bags or rolls of 100-1,000 Mexican, Austrian, or South African coins, but these would usually have to be ordered specially. Many dealers prefer to sell in quantities of not less than ten coins, and often their advertisements quote prices only for orders of 10 coins or more.

The real attraction of the gold coins, however, is to the small investor who wants to buy perhaps one or two at a time, costing him a few hundred dollars.

All gold coins carry some premium over their gold content. This is lowest (anything from 5% to 15% usually) on legal tender coins or restrikes in current production; highest on coins like the U.S. $20 double eagle, which has not been made officially (though it is faked) for almost fifty years. Basically, the restrikes and the Krugerrand are known as bullion coins; sovereigns and U.S. double eagles are trade coins.

No gold coins are *pure* gold. Most are 900 or 916.6 fine gold; the purest are the Austrian 1 and 4 ducat coins, which are 986.6 fine. A designation of 916.6 fine means that a coin is 11/12 fine gold and 1/12 alloy.

The main gold coins, listed in ascending weights, are:

1. Austrian 1 Ducat 1915

0.1109 ounce fine gold content

986.6 fine

This delicate little Austrian coin, the lightest in general circulation in the U.S., is what is known as an official restrike. This coin, along with the 20 crown, 4 ducat, and 100 crown (listed below), is currently made at the government Mint in Vienna to meet orders placed by leading banks and bullion dealers. All coins are dated 1915, the last year of the old Austro-Hungarian Empire, and they are copies of the traditional gold coins that circulated in the days of the Empire. The 1 ducat coin bears the garlanded head of Emperor

Franz-Joseph on one side, and the arms of the old Austro-Hungarian Empire on the other.

Because they are minted more or less to meet demand, the 1 ducat coins, together with the other Austrian restrikes, command only a modest premium over their gold content, to cover striking costs, handling, and dealers' charges. The premium is usually between 8% and 12%, but may go lower or higher according to demand. The premium was down to 5% for a while in October 1974.

Certainly this coin represents one of the cheapest ways to buy gold. Even with a gold price of $200, a single coin should cost only about $27.

2.   Austrian 20 Crown 1915

0.1960 ounce fine gold content

900 fine

Like the 1 ducat described above, this coin is a restrike, but it is not such pure gold as the 1 ducat; this one is only 900 fine. However, it is another good buy if your gold-buying budget is limited, because it does not command much premium over the gold content; usually it will be between 8% and 12%. The coins were selling for around $36 each late in October 1974 (with gold at just under $160) and would still cost only about $46 with a $200 gold price. Good discounts are available on bulk buying of a coin like this. One leading dealer was quoting $36.30 for the single coin in late October 1974, but $355 for ten coins ($35.50 each), or

$3,500 ($35 each) for orders of one hundred coins.

3. British Sovereign
0.2354 ounces fine gold content
916.66 fine

This famous gold coin was first struck by King George III in 1817. Originally it was equal in value to £1 sterling ($2.33 at today's exchange rates), but it now retails anywhere between $50 and $70, depending on the gold price.

Minting of the sovereign continued right through the nineteenth century and up to the present day. The coin bears the head of the current monarch on one side, and the reverse depicts St. George slaying a dragon. Coins bearing the head of the young Queen Victoria, and of the old Queen Victoria (known as "widows") still circulate, but you will find most commonly the sovereigns dated 1902-1933 bearing the heads of either Edward VII or George V. There are also "new" sovereigns bearing the head of Queen Elizabeth II. The latest large minting of Queen Elizabeth sovereigns took place in 1968, but a new batch was being struck in 1974 and has just arrived on the market.

Although over 300 million of these coins have been struck, they command a considerable rarity premium. On the older sovereigns the premium is now close to 50%, while on Queen Elizabeths it was running at just over 50% late in 1974.

This does make the sovereign a relatively expensive

coin to buy, considering it contains less than ¼ ounce of gold, but it is certainly a good buy if you have less than $100 to spend. Moreover, it is a current coin, unlike the restrikes from Austria, which are merely copies of old ones.

4.   Austrian 4 Ducat 1915
0.4438 ounce fine gold content
986.6 fine

This large, thin coin, with an exceptionally high luster, is perhaps the most spectacular of the Austrian restrikes. And if you are eager to own a gold coin that is the closest thing to pure gold then this is it; it is 986.6 parts per thousand pure gold. The coin shows the garlanded head and shoulders of Emperor Franz-Joseph.

As on all the Austrian restrikes, the premium is usually modest, and you should be able to buy it for about $100 even with a gold price of $200.

5.   Mexican 20 Pesos 1959
0.4823 ounce fine gold content
900 fine

This "restrike" gold coin contains almost exactly half an ounce of fine gold, and it is thus easy to calculate its price by dividing the day's gold price in two and adding about a 10% premium. The coins are being currently minted in Mexico by the official Mint and are issued by the Bank of Mexico. The Bank is marketing them through two leading New York dealers, Mocatta Metals Corporation and Republic National Bank of

New York, and through one Swiss bank. The premium is usually between 10% and 15% over the gold content. So with gold at $200 an ounce, they would cost just over $100.

6. U.S. $20 Double Eagle
0.9675 ounce fine gold content
900 fine

This most famous of American gold coins was first issued for general circulation in 1850. Until 1907 it carried the head of "Miss Liberty," and so is often known as the Liberty Head. It was redesigned in 1907 by sculptor Augustus Saint-Gaudens, who changed the design to the standing figure of "Liberty"; the coin was then rechristened the St. Gaudens. The reverse of both the Liberty Head and the St. Gaudens depict the American Eagle, and most issues bear the words IN GOD WE TRUST. The coin has not been struck since 1932. Nowadays the most commonly found coins are dated between 1895 and 1928, and you will usually not be able to specify the date you require.

The Double Eagle is widely hoarded in France, the Middle East, and Eastern Europe. And it has been extensively faked, especially in Italy and Lebanon. You should be careful to buy this coin only from reputable dealers, who are generally eagle-eyed at sorting out fakes from the real thing.

Because it has not been minted in the U.S. for over 40 years, it does have a rarity value and commands a high premium. During much of 1974 the premium was over 80%. It is, therefore, an expensive coin to buy, and may cost you well over $300 with a gold price of $200.

However, it is quite possible that once gold ownership is legalized in the U.S., the premium will come down because of the many other forms of gold holding open to everyone. In recent years the Double Eagle has been one of the few gold coins Americans could hold legally, so this has enhanced its value. Before rushing out to buy it, you should watch to see how the premium is reacting to general gold ownership. It would be a pity to buy it with an 80% premium, if that were to drop in a few months' time. On the other hand, the coin does have genuine historical value, as compared with the Mexican and Austrian restrikes, which ultimately may be worth only their remelt value.

(The other best-known American gold coins are the $10 Eagle Liberty, $10 Indian, and $5 Liberty, but as the premium on these coins is sometimes 100% they are not being discussed in this book for the general gold investor. They are more of collectors' items, and you should seek specialist literature at your coin dealers.)

7.   Austrian 100 Crown 1915
0.9802 ounce fine gold content
900 fine

This is the best known of the Austrian coins and, like the 1 and 4 ducat and 20 crown described above, is a restrike currently made at the Mint in Vienna. It is dated 1915. The coins have been very popular in West

Germany, Austria, and Eastern Europe for more than a decade and have been permitted to circulate in the United States since the beginning of 1974. They command a relatively small premium over their gold content, usually 10%-12% at retail level, but sometimes much less. The premium was down to 5% late in 1974.

Since they contain just under one ounce of fine gold, the premium usually brings their price up to only just over the day's international gold price. So if you know the gold price, you can judge that an Austrian 100 crown will cost you only a few dollars more.

8. Hungarian 100 Crown 1915
0.9802 ounce fine gold content
900 fine

When the U.S. regulations on gold holding were first eased in January 1974 to permit the import of restrikes, the demand for Austrian 100 Crowns was so great that the Mint in Vienna could not cope. So one enterprising bullion dealer, Republic National Bank of New York, persuaded the official Mint in Budapest to start making a Hungarian version of the old 100-crown coin of the Austro-Hungarian Empire. The coin has the same specifications of weight and gold content as the Austrian one and is usually traded at the same price.

9. South African Krugerrand
1.0 ounce fine gold content
916.66 fine

The Krugerrand is unique in that it has a fine gold

content of exactly one ounce. The coin was first struck by the South African Mint in 1967 and was minted in that year and in 1968 and 1969 in limited numbers of "proof" quality, and sold in South Africa on the basis of one coin per person at a relatively high premium. But since 1970 it has been struck in increasing quantities and sold widely in Europe at a low premium of 8% over gold content. The South Africans, being the world's largest gold producers, see the coin as the ideal way for the ordinary person to buy a small quantity of gold. And since it contains one ounce of the metal, the price parallels very closely the daily gold price.

Since 1970, when the coin was first actively marketed, almost 5-million Krugerrands have been sold, and production in 1975 is expected to be up to 150,000 every week, taking up almost one-third of all the Republic's gold output. The coins have so far proved most popular in West Germany and Britain, where, because they are classed as legal tender coins (unlike the Austrian and Mexican restrikes) they are exempt from sales taxes. In 1975 they will be available in the U.S. for the first time.

The coins show the head of President Kruger on one side, and a South African springbok and the words *Fyngoud 1 oz fine gold* on the reverse. The coins on sale in the U.S. will largely be dated 1974 and 1975.

The premium over the gold content should be about 8% but may well rise to 10% or even higher at the retail level. During the autumn of 1974 the demand for the coins was so high that the premium went up over 15%.

The appeal of the Krugerrand is simply that if you want to own just one ounce of fine gold, this is the easiest way to do it.

10.   Mexican 50 Pesos 1947
1.2057 ounces fine gold content
900 fine

This large gold coin was first issued in 1921 to mark the 100th anniversary of Mexico's independence. It is known, therefore, as the "centenario." Since the end of World War II the coin has been regularly restruck by the Mint in Mexico City and issued through the Bank of Mexico. The centenario has been widely traded in Europe, especially in Paris, where it is traded daily in the special gold-dealing room of the Bourse. The coin also circulates widely in South America, where it is the most popular with hoarders. Americans have been permitted to hold the 50-pesos coins since the beginning of 1974, and an active market has already been established.

The coin, designed by Emilio del Moral, shows the Mexican coat of arms of an eagle and a snake on one side, with a Winged Victory on the reverse before the outline of the two famous Mexican volcanos Popocatapetl and Ixtlaccihuatl. Round the edge of the coin the words Independencia y Libertad are inscribed. All coins are dated 1947.

Since the coin is currently minted to meet demand the premium is usually low, and should be between 10% and 15% over gold content. But its sheer weight does make it an expensive coin. With gold at $200 you could expect to pay $260 or more for it.

TABLE 4
QUICK GUIDE TO GOLD COIN PRICES° IN $

Gold Price:	$125	$150	$175	$200	$225	$250
Austrian 1 Ducat	15	18	21	24	27	30
Austrian 20 Crown	27	32	38	43	49	54
British Sovereign	44	53	62	71	79	88
Austrian 4 Ducat	61	73	85	98	111	122
Mexican 20 Peso	66	80	93	106	119	133
US $20 Double Eagle	218	261	305	348	392	435
Austrian 100 Crown	135	162	189	216	243	275
Hungarian 100 Crown	135	162	189	216	243	275
South African Krugerrand	137	165	192	220	247	275
Mexican 50 Pesos	166	199	232	265	298	332

°All prices are approximate, and include 10% premium on all coins, except Sovereigns, where the premium is calculated at 50%, and the US $20 Double Eagle, where it is set at 80%.

7 Gold Bars for All Pockets

The real novelty for Americans in 1975 is the opportunity to buy bars of gold for the first time. They come in all sizes to suit all pockets. The smallest bars—wafers, really—weigh ½ ounce, the largest are the 400-ounce "good delivery" bars that are traded on the international market. In between are at least eight other bar sizes.

You can expect to encounter the following weights:

½	ounce
1	ounce
5	ounces
10	ounces
½	kilo (16.075 ounces)
25	ounces
1	kilo (32.15 ounces)
50	ounces
100	ounces
400	ounces

In practice, however, only the smaller bars up to 1 kilo are likely to be widely displayed. The larger bars will be chiefly held by major dealers for investors and will be traded on the gold futures markets (described in Chapter 12).

The bars are of two types. First, the ½-ounce and 1-ounce bars are coined bars. They are made of rolled sheets of gold stamped out to be of an exact weight, and then struck with a 200-400 ton press to mark details of the bar's weight, fineness, and the name of the approved issuer. Actually, the strike compresses the portion of the bar *not* bearing the legend, so the details appear raised. This method is a safeguard against counterfeiting as it is hard to achieve outside professional mints. These coined bars will usually be sold over the counter in the U.S. in little plastic packets.

The second type of bar is the cast bar, which is

poured from melted gold, then filed to exact weight. All cast bars are stamped with the weight, fineness, name of the approved issuer and a *serial number* (the coined bars do *not* have serial numbers).

The fineness of the bar indicates its purity. To be "good delivery" on world markets a bar must be at least 995 parts per thousand pure gold. The bars you will see on sale in the United States, will be of varied purities, but always *at least* 995. The ½-ounce and 1-ounce coined bars, and the cast 5-ounce will be 999.5 (i.e., of exceptionally high purity), while the 10-ounce and kilo bars will generally be either 995 or 999.9 (but you may also see some stamped 999). The 100-ounce bars will come in 995 and 999.5.

The higher purity bars are made primarily for specialist use in industry and jewelery, and if you are buying bars for investment or speculation you will do just as well with 995 purity. There is always an extra premium on bars of 999.5 or 999.9 quality, because they have to be refined up to this purity by a costly electrolytic process. (Incidentally, the Russians always sell 999.9 gold and for that reason Russian bars command a slightly higher price than South African, which are usually 995 or 996.) So, given a choice, buy 995 bars; it will be cheaper, and any profits you make will not normally be affected.

The other crucial detail to look for on a bar, beside the weight and fineness, is the name of the refiner who made it, or the issuer. Turning out gold bars of a constant high standard is a special art. The elite of these bar makers are the 49 refiners and assayers in 14 countries (ranging from the U.S. and Canada, to Britain, the Soviet Union, and China) whose bars are approved by the London gold market. They include three in the United States, and four in Canada.

In practice, you will only see the names of a limited number of these firms, and instead of their name (or sometimes with) you may also find that of a leading bank or bullion dealer. In the United States you are most likely to see bars of the following refiners.

> Engelhard
> Handy & Harman
> Matthey-Bishop
> Johnson Matthey (London)
> Canadian Copper Refineries (Montreal)
> Compagnie des Metaux Precieux (Paris)
> Argor S.A. (Switzerland)
> Valcambi S.A. (Switzerland)
> Degussa (West Germany)

This list covers simply the major North American and European suppliers. It is not definitive, and the fact that a firm is not included here does not mean that its bars are in any way less good.

You will not see either South African or Russian bars directly, because they make only 400-ounce "good delivery" bars, which are remelted into small bars by European or North American refiners. But the small bars you buy may well be made up of South African or Russian gold.

In addition you may see bars bearing the names of such major banks and bullion dealers as:

> Mocatta and Goldsmid
> Bank of Nova Scotia
> Rothschild
> Sharps Pixley
> Swiss Bank Corporation
> Swiss Credit Bank
> Union Bank of Switzerland

Again this is not a definitive listing, but it includes the "brands" most likely to be encountered.

Moreover, all the major refiners and dealers will be endeavoring to create the best possible "image" for their bars during the first few months of American buying. As the gold dealer at Engelhard, one of the leading U.S. bar makers, emphasized to me, "We hope to create an image of quality and class for our bars; to make people feel that buying one of them is like buying a diamond at Tiffany's. We stand behind the name on our bars forever."

The actual price of the bars will always be closely allied to the London fixing price (see Chapter 4), but on the smaller bars there will be a considerable premium over the gold content to cover the extra costs of making them (it is obviously much cheaper to make one 400 ounce "good delivery" bar than 400 one-ounce wafers). The premium on the ½-ounce, 1-ounce, and 5-ounce bars is expected to be at least 5% and perhaps up to 8%. If you are buying the ½-ounce or 1-ounce bars over the counter in some specialty shops or department stores you may pay even more than that.

But marketing will be very competitive, and some dealers anticipate that the Swiss banks, in particular, will try to sell small bars at a very low premium to capture a good slice of the new market. So shop around for small bars; you will certainly find some variations in price.

If you are setting out to buy a gold bar (or several) you should consider carefully just why you are buying. If you want to get some ½-ounce or 1-ounce bars as personal souvenirs to give to grandchildren or other relatives for birthdays or Christmas, then by all means go ahead. But if you are buying just a few hundred dollars worth of gold yourself for investment or because you wish to keep a small slice of your savings in gold, then you may prefer to buy gold coins. The small gold bars will only be bought back by dealers or banks, subject to assay (that is to say, testing to see they are genuine). And even then they will not really be interested in buying back just one or two little bars—the paperwork involved is not worth it. With gold coins, however, it is much easier to walk into a coin shop and sell them direct.

The larger gold bars, from 10-ounce up, and especially the kilo bar and the 100-ounce bar, are ideal for

TABLE 5
QUICK GUIDE TO GOLD BAR PRICES° IN $

Gold Price:	$125	$150	$175	$200	$225	$250
½ ounce	67	81	94	108	121	135
1 ounce	135	162	189	216	243	270
5 ounces	675	810	945	1080	1215	1350
10 ounces	1312	1575	1837	2100	2362	2625
½ kilo (16.075 ounces)	2070	2484	2898	3311	3725	4139
25 ounces	3219	3862	4506	5150	5794	6437
1 kilo (32.15 ounces)	4099	4919	5739	6559	7378	8198
50 ounces	6375	7650	8925	10200	11475	12750
100 ounces	12500	15000	17500	20000	22500	25000
400 ounces	50000	60000	70000	80000	90000	100000

°All prices are approximate, and include premiums as follows:

		1 kilo	
	10 ounces: 5%	50 Ounces } 2%	
½ ounce ⎤			
1 ounce } 8%	½ kilo } 3%	100 ounces } Nil	
5 ounces ⎦	25 ounces	400 ounces	

investing in gold because they all carry serial numbers and will be easier to sell back (although possibly still subject to assay if you take delivery). The premium on these bars will also be less. Dealers are anticipating a premium of 3% on the kilo bar, but this is much higher than has been customary in Europe, and it may settle at 1%-2%.

On the 995 fine 100-ounce and 400-ounce bars there

is no premium over gold content, and the only additional charges should be any freight, insurance, and dealers' handling charges involved.

One final word of warning. Be sure you buy gold bars only from first-class banks and highly reputable dealers. A fake gold bar (or one without the right gold content) can be hard even for an expert to detect without scientific equipment. There are tales in the Far East that expert Chinese dealers can tell a bar's true gold content just by rubbing it on a special stone, but that is not recommended for beginners. So buy from a quality dealer and check for those basic three marks of weight, fineness, and issuer's or refiner's name on every bar; bars of 5 ounces or over will also most likely have a serial number.

8 Safeguarding Your Gold

So you have bought your gold bars or gold coins. How to keep them safely? The best possible policy is not to take delivery of them in the first place. That may seem contradictory at first glance, but it is the wisest course both in terms of safety and in the interests of reselling.

Let's look at safety first. If you take the gold home, what do you do with it? Traditionally, European peasants have stuffed it under mattresses or buried it in the garden. And I suppose there is no reason why the average American citizen should not squirrel it away likewise. But remember that burglars know from long experience all the best hiding places in the average home (though they may not have time to dig up the garden). Even if you have a safe, that is not inviolable. Also, those Europeans who took the gold home were often doing it when their country was threatened by invasion (the French, twice in a generation); since that prospect does not face the U.S., then the real need to have gold at home is gone. If you do still take it home and want to insure it, your insurance company will almost certainly insist you keep it in a safe or return it to a bank safe-deposit box. So you might as well have left it with the bank in the first place.

My advice is that if you do take delivery, put the gold in a bank safety-deposit box. It is foolish to keep it around the home, and, if word got out, might even lure burglars. And if it is stolen it is unlikely to be recovered, because it can be remelted easily and all marks (like serial numbers) destroyed.

Clearly this does not apply to the odd ½-ounce or 1-ounce bar you may buy as a souvenir or present. You will obviously want to keep that at home. But just remember that although it looks a tiny slip of metal, it is still worth anything between $150 and $200 at current prices. Don't leave it lying around.

Now, if you leave the gold with a bank or dealer you have several advantages. First, some may store it at no charge, or only a modest annual fee. Merrill Lynch, for example, have announced that they will hold gold for clients for up to six months at no charge at all (provided you bought it from them) and thereafter at a minimal charge for storage and insurance. Other dealers are quoting storage charges of ½ % per year or less (i.e., 50 cents on every $100 worth of gold). Since this leaves you free of *all* worries about looking after it, it is a small price to pay. Probably cheaper than renting a safe-deposit box.

The other great advantage in leaving the gold with a bank or leading dealer is that if you want to sell it, you will be able to do so immediately. If you have taken delivery of the gold, even just to put it in your safe-deposit box at the bank where you made the purchase, it will only be bought back subject to assay. And in that situation you will not receive payment until the assay is complete (which may take some days), and the price you get will reflect the cost of assay (which may be $75-$150 per bar). On the other hand, gold left with a bank or dealer, in their own custody, can be sold instantly.

Clearly, if you wish to trade in gold at all, you should leave it with the bank.

9 Fakes and Frauds

Coins

Faking gold coins has long been a profitable business, especially in Italy and Beirut, so that today there are millions of fake coins in circulation. The forgers have turned their skill primarily towards coins like the U.S. $20 double eagle, the British sovereign, and the French 20-franc Napoleon, which command a considerable premium over their gold content. The forger's profit, in fact, comes from that premium, for many fake coins contain precisely the right amount of gold and are very hard to detect from the real thing. For this reason the faking of Austrian restrikes or the Krugerrand is less profitable, because they attract low premiums; they are not (as yet) faked much, if at all.

The best advice is to be sure to buy coins only from highly reputable dealers, who will usually inspect all coins they sell very carefully to detect fakes. In your day-to-day coin buying the coins to be most careful of are the double eagles, and the British sovereigns with the heads of Edward VII and George V (since the latter are faked in the Middle East where, for religious reasons, many people will not accept a coin with a female head). But to the uneducated eye they are hard to sort out from the real thing. So it is in your own interest to establish a good relationship with a reliable coin dealer or coin-dealing bank.

What happens if you do get stuck with some fake coins? Well, they will still probably have about the right gold content, and you should be able to sell them for their "remelt value." The price you get will be less than the gold price of the day, but at least you will not suffer a complete loss. Before selling back possible fakes for remelt value, however, be sure to check with several dealers.

Gold Bars

The advice here is simple; buy only from first-class banks or dealers, and be sure that the bars bear the right stamps of weight, fineness, and issuer (as described in Chapter 7). Of course, a fake can have false details on it too, and you should never be tempted by special offers of gold bars at cut-rate prices under the prevailing gold price.

Gold dealers the world over are constantly plagued by a number of fraudulent operators trying to sell them gold at three or four dollars an ounce under the prevailing price. These operators usually explain that the gold is part of a long-lost hoard or is the property of some South American dictator. They may even show one or two completely genuine bars in trying to con the dealers into putting up money for the rest. No doubt there will be all kinds of similar attempts to persuade the American public, newly allowed to own gold, to buy some fake bars too. So, be highly suspicious of anyone, other than an established bank or dealer, trying to sell you gold—especially if it is a "special offer" below the day's gold price. You may think you can save money—but you will not.

Beware also of vague newspaper or magazine advertisements offering "gold ingots" at tempting prices. There are already some cases before the courts of fraudulent companies with very fancy sounding names being set up to persuade people to buy silver bars. These companies advertised in newspapers giving P.O. Box numbers to which checks were to be mailed. They simply collected the checks and vanished into the night; they never sent an ounce of silver.

So you should be wary of newspaper advertisements. Many will be placed, of course, by entirely legitimate bullion and coin dealers and you need have no fear of dealing with them. But before mailing money to any dealer, do check out their authenticity and discuss the purchase with them by phone. And, if in doubt, ask your bank to handle the purchase of gold for you. The point is that a network of entirely trustworthy outlets is being set up (see Chapter 5, Where to Buy) and you will save yourself both worry—and money—if you go directly to them.

10 Investing in Gold-Selected Portfolios

How much of your assets should you put into gold?
And what sort of gold portfolio should you build up?

In European countries in the last two or three years
there has been a trend toward putting perhaps 10%-
15% of liquid assets into gold. Many banks have been
advising their clients to have at least that much in gold
as a hedge against currency devaluations. Americans,
initially, may not wish to switch so much into gold, but
this is a good guide to what has been happening across

the Atlantic. The amount you will wish to invest in gold will depend very much on how you or your broker view the future of the dollar. If you fear future devaluations, then you may wish to go for up to 15%. Your investment in gold will also obviously depend on the state of Wall Street. With the stock market in the doldrums during 1974, gold suddenly seems a bright alternative, but if Wall Street picks up in 1975, then gold's lure might wane. In practice, the amount you invest in gold will depend on what other good prospects are around at the time.

Now, what sort of portfolio should you assemble? The investor with several thousand dollars to switch into gold has a choice of three main ways of going about it. He can buy gold bullion bars or coin, he can buy shares in a gold bullion fund, or he can play the gold futures markets. This chapter looks at the first two of these choices; Chapter 12 describes the futures markets.

The important point in buying physical gold is to allow yourself the maximum flexibility to indulge in a little profit-taking from time to time. If you have all your money tied up in one 400-ounce bar, costing perhaps $80,000, then you have to dispose of that to realize any profit at all. Consider, therefore, buying perhaps three 100-ounce bars and three kilo bars, which would cost about the same, but also provide the opportunity of selling either a single kilo bar or a 100-ounce bar at a time.

The serious investor is going to consider not only how to buy his gold, but also how to ensure the best liquidity when he wants to sell. Leading dealers suggest that the ideal position is to hold between 2,000 and 4,000 ounces of gold (i.e., 5 to 10 "good delivery" bars), which would cost $400,000 to $800,000 with gold at $200 an ounce. In the first place there will normally be no transaction cost in selling this gold, whereas sales of smaller amounts may attract a cost of $50-$60. Secondly, to try to sell *more* gold than this at any moment could affect the price adversely. This does not mean that you cannot hold more than 4,000 ounces of gold; merely that if you do you should be aware that it might not be wise to sell it all at once.

Let's look at some specific portfolios. Suppose you have $25,000 to invest in gold. At a gold price of $200 you could put this into, say, 3 kilo bars (about $6,559 each), which would cost you nearly $20,000; then perhaps two 10-ounce bars at just over $2,000 each; that leaves around $1,000 that could be put into gold coins —perhaps 5 Krugerrand, or 10 Austrian 4 ducat. This gives you reasonable flexibility to sell the occasional bar or a few coins to take advantage of a price rise.

If you have $100,000 to invest, with the gold price at $200, then you could opt either for one 400-ounce bar at $80,000, together with $20,000 worth of smaller bars (say 3 kilo bars), or for greater flexibility, take five 100-ounce bars at $20,000 each. (Tables 6-11 give selected portfolios up to $1 million.)

Having chosen how much you wish to buy, the next question is the precise way in which you buy it. You can, of course, buy the physical gold and store it yourself. But, as I have already suggested, this can be both expensive and inconvenient because you will not only pay extra freight and insurance in taking delivery, but there may be delays in selling back the gold. The best choice is to have the gold held for you by the bullion dealer or an approved warehouse, where storage charges will normally be about ½% per year.

Now, if you decide not to take delivery, then you have several options. You can buy the gold at your local bank, or with a New York dealer. You can also buy gold for delivery at a bullion broker's or bank's vault in London or Switzerland. If you do this there will normally be no premium over the London gold price, except ¼% commission if your gold is bought at the "fixing" (outside of fixing, the dealer makes you his own price, which includes his commission). The advantage here is that you have complete liquidity and can sell it again without commission. Your gold, in fact, never comes into the United States at all.

An alternative choice is to buy a "Delivery Order," a gold certificate, if you like, issued by a specific bullion dealer. Firms such as Mocatta Metals Corporation will be issuing these Delivery Orders both for gold bullion and coin. The Delivery Orders will be for gold held in storage at recognized precious metal warehouses in the U.S. and Switzerland. The Delivery Orders will be transferable and have the advantage that they do *not* attract sales tax. They will be accepted both by the issuing bullion dealer and by other leading dealers. If you wish to consider this form of gold purchase, your local bank or one of the main dealers listed in the Gold Buyer's Address Book will give you more details.

While the investor with several hundred thousand (or million) dollars at his disposal may prefer to deal directly with major bullion dealers, other investors will find that brokerage firms will also be able to handle their purchases for them.

One of the most complete networks for the investor is being established by Merrill Lynch, Pierce, Fenner & Smith, Inc. To facilitate gold investing, they have set up a joint company with Handy and Harman, one of the leading American precious metals fabricators, and Samuel Montagu & Co., one of the five members of the London gold market. The new company is called Merrill, Montagu and Handy and Harman. Montagu's will procure and trade bullion on world markets for the new company; Handy and Harman will fabricate the gold bullion bars; and Merrill Lynch will be offering gold to U.S. institutions and citizens, at both wholesale and retail level, through all their 262 offices in the U.S. Merrill Lynch say they will accept minimum orders of 5 ounces or more ($1,000 at $200 gold price) from private individuals.

Announcing their plans, Merrill Lynch stated: "Customers of Merrill Lynch will be able to call their account executives to purchase the gold. All gold transactions will be made in cash accounts. If the purchaser leaves the metal with Merrill Lynch, ownership will be listed on his regular customer account statements."

Moreover, if the gold is left in Merrill Lynch's custody they will be able to resell it instantly, usually at the London price for the following morning, less their handling charge.

Other leading brokerage firms will be offering very similar facilities, and you should check with your broker for the precise arrangements he offers.

The New York Stock Exchange is also considering making a secondary market for spot gold.

Some leading banks will also be offering regular gold investment facilities. And, provided you leave the gold with them, they may be prepared to let you buy on margin. Since the gold price is very volatile nowadays this margin would probably be considerable (over 25%). Alternatively, many banks will be prepared to make loans provided they hold your gold as collateral. In fact, one good reason for many banks to get into gold trading will be the ancillary business that it will bring in terms of loans to customers.

The opportunities are also being widened for gold investment through the creation of several gold funds, in which an investor simply purchases shares. The assets of the fund are then invested in gold bullion. The advantage here, of course, is that the ordinary investor is relieved of all worries of actually buying or selling physical gold.

One major fund already launched is Bars of Gold, Inc., a new company sponsored by Calvin Bullock Ltd., and underwritten by Bache & Co. Inc., Paine, Webber, Jackson & Curtis Inc., E.F. Hutton & Company Inc., and Reynolds Securities Inc. The Company will operate like a mutual fund by selling and redeeming its shares at net asset value based on the daily London gold-fixing price. Bars of Gold plans to raise an initial $105 million through an initial offering of common stock. Minimum purchase was set at 100 shares at $15 a piece (i.e., minimum stake $1,500), and subsequent purchases in lots of 50 shares. The stock will be redeemable in U.S. dollars, Swiss francs, or gold bullion.

The initial $105 million will be invested principally in 400-ounce bars, bought on the open market and stored with U.S. and Swiss banks. Launching the fund, the company's treasurer explained its purpose was "to

TABLE 6
WHAT YOU CAN BUY FOR UNDER $100

When the Gold Price is:

$150	$200	$250
Austrian 1 Ducat ($18)	Austrian 1 Ducat ($24)	Austrian 1 Ducat ($30)
Austrian 20 Crown ($32)	Austrian 20 Crown ($43)	Austrian 20 Crown ($54)
British Sovereign ($53)	British Sovereign ($71)	British Sovereign ($88)
Austrian 4 Ducat ($73)	Austrian 4 Ducat ($98)	____
Mexican 20 Peso ($80)	____	____

TABLE 7
WHAT YOU CAN BUY FOR $500

When the gold price is:

$150	**$200**	**$250**
Austrian 1 Ducat ($18)	Austrian 1 Ducat ($24)	Austrian 1 Ducat ($30)
Austrian 20 Crown ($32)	Austrian 20 Crown ($43)	Austrian 20 Crown ($54)
British Sovereign ($53)	British Sovereign ($71)	British Sovereign ($88)
Austrian 4 Ducat ($73)	Austrian 4 Ducat ($98)	Austrian 4 Ducat ($122)
Mexican 20 Peso ($80)	Mexican 20 Peso ($106)	Mexican 20 Peso ($133)
US $20 Double Eagle ($261)	US $20 Double Eagle ($348)	US $20 Double Eagle ($435)
Austrian 100 Crown ($162)	Austrian 100 Crown ($216)	Austrian 100 Crown ($275)
Hungarian 100 Crown ($162)	Hungarian 100 Crown ($216)	Hungarian 100 Crown ($275)
SA Krugerrand ($165)	SA Krugerrand ($220)	SA Krugerrand ($275)
Mexican 50 Peso ($199)	Mexican 50 Peso ($265)	Mexican 50 Peso ($332)
½-ounce bar ($81)	½-ounce bar ($108)	½-ounce bar ($135)
1-ounce bar ($162)	1-ounce bar ($216)	1-ounce ($270)

make it convenient to own gold without having to buy and store bars."

During the first year of gold ownership, other gold bullion funds will be launched and you should watch

TABLE 8
WHAT YOU CAN BUY FOR UNDER $10000

When the gold price is:

$150	$200	$250
Austrian 1 Ducat ($18)	Austrian 1 Ducat ($24)	Austrian 1 Ducat ($30)
Austrian 20 Crown ($32)	Austrian 20 Crown ($43)	Austrian 20 Crown ($54)
British Sovereign ($53)	British Sovereign ($71)	British Sovereign ($88)
Austrian 4 Ducat ($73)	Austrian 4 Ducat ($98)	Austrian 4 Ducat ($122)
Mexican 20 Peso ($80)	Mexican 20 Peso ($106)	Mexican 20 Peso ($133)
US $20 Double Eagle ($261)	US $20 Double Eagle ($348)	US $20 Double Eagle ($435)
Austrian 100 Crown ($162)	Austrian 100 Crown ($216)	Austrian 100 Crown ($275)
Hungarian 100 Crown ($162)	Hungarian 100 Crown ($216)	Hungarian 100 Crown ($275)
SA Krugerrand ($165)	SA Krugerrand ($220)	SA Krugerrand ($275)
Mexican 50 Peso ($199)	Mexican 50 Peso ($265)	Mexican 50 Peso ($332)
½-ounce bar ($81)	½-ounce bar ($108)	½-ounce bar ($135)
1-ounce bar ($162)	1-ounce bar ($216)	1-ounce bar ($270)
5-ounce bar ($810)	____	____

the financial press or business pages of newspapers for details.

TABLE 9
HOW YOU COULD INVEST WHEN GOLD IS $150

Amount to Invest			
$5,000	1 kilo bar ($4,900) + balance in small coins	*or*	1 ½-kilo bar ($2,500) + 1 10-ounce bar ($1,600) + balance in small coins
$10,000	1 kilo bar ($4,900) + 2 ½-kilo bars ($5,000)	*or*	2 kilo bars ($9,800) + balance in small coins
$25,000	5 kilo bars ($24,600) + balance in small coins	*or*	1 100-ounce bar ($15,000) + 2 kilo bars ($9,800) + balance in small coins
$50,000	3 100-ounce bars ($45,000) + 1 kilo bar ($4,900)	*or*	2 100-ounce bars $30,000) + 4 kilo bars ($19,700)
$100,000	1 400-ounce bar ($60,000) + 8 kilo bars ($39,400)	*or*	5 100-ounce bars ($75,000) + 5 kilo bars ($24,600)
$1,000,000	16 400-ounce bars ($960,000) + 8 kilo bars ($39,400)		

The advantage of such funds is that they do offer an investor with just a few thousand dollars a chance to benefit from really large-scale gold buying. Of course, the fund does charge an annual management fee (listed to date at about 0.31 of 1%), and you have to pray that the fund's gold-buying policy is a wise one. There is also the snag of double taxation; the fund has to pay tax on its profits, the investor also has to pay tax on his. You should check with a fund in advance precisely what the tax liabilities are likely to be.

The other option, for someone with a little more of a gambler's instinct, is to play the gold futures markets.

TABLE 10
HOW YOU COULD INVEST WHEN GOLD IS $200

**Amount
to Invest**

$5,000	2 10-ounce bars ($4,200) + balance in small coins	*or*	1 ½-kilo bar ($3,300) + 1 5-ounce bar ($1,100) + balance in small coins
$10,000	1 kilo bar ($6,600) + 1 10-ounce bar ($2,100) + balance in small coins	*or*	3 ½-kilo bars ($10,000)
$25,000	3 kilo bars ($19,700) + 2 10-ounce bars ($4,200) + balance in small coins	*or*	2 50-ounce bars ($20,400) + 1 ½-kilo bar ($3,300) + balance in small coins
$50,000	2 100-ounce bars ($40,000) + 3 ½-kilo bars ($10,000)	*or*	7 kilo bars ($45,900) + balance in small coins
$100,000	1 400-ounce bar ($80,000) +3 kilo bars ($20,000)	*or*	5 100-ounce bars ($100,000)
$1,000,000	12 400-ounce bars ($960,000) + 2 100-ounce bars ($40,000)		

TABLE 11
HOW YOU COULD INVEST WHEN GOLD IS $250

Amount to Invest			
$5,000	1 ½-kilo bar ($4,100) + balance in small coins	*or*	1 10-ounce bar ($2,600) + 1 5-ounce bar ($1,300) balance in small coins
$10,000	1 kilo bar ($8,200) + 1 5-ounce bar ($1,300) + balance in small coins	*or*	3 10-ounce bars ($7,900) +1 5-ounce bar ($1,300) + balance in small coins
$25,000	1 100-ounce bar ($25,000)	*or*	3 kilo bars ($24,600) + balance in small coins
$50,000	2 100-ounce bars ($50,000)	*or*	1 100-ounce bar ($25,000) + 3 kilo bars ($24,600)
$100,000	1 400-ounce bar ($100,000)	*or*	3 100-ounce bars ($75,000) + 3 kilo bars ($24,600)
		or	4 100-ounce bars ($100,000)
$1,000,000	10 400-ounce bars ($1,000,000)		

11 Corporate Buying

For the first time in a generation, gold has become a serious consideration for corporate investment. Faced with falling stock markets and weak currencies, many commercial banks, multi-national companies, and even mutual funds in Europe and Canada have felt it prudent to switch at least part of their liquid assets into gold during 1973 and 1974. Their treasurers, viewing the uncertain international monetary horizon, have felt that a modest position in gold is a wise hedge against currency devaluations. Furthermore, for companies doing much international business, gold can be a useful part of their foreign exchange holdings. Even British firms, who would have scoffed at the notion of buying gold a few years ago, have taken a sudden fancy in 1974 to the Krugerrand gold coins (the British may not hold gold bullion) and have been buying them in quantities of 5,000 to 10,000 at a time. This policy has been dictated not so much by the possibility of a price rise, but through fear of further devaluations of sterling and a dismal stock market. And their new faith in gold has sometimes been swiftly rewarded. One company made a 20% profit on its investment in Krugerrand in just seven weeks.

Clearly American companies—and banks—will review this European experience in devising their own strategy toward gold.

The two most immediate areas to consider will be whether to hold some gold either as part of foreign exchange positions and/or as part of investment portfolios. The question of whether to put trust or pension funds into gold will almost certainly be considered later, once an organization has experience in some other gold dealings. There is also the tricky legal question with regard to trust funds of whether, under the "prudent man" rule, funds can actually be diverted into gold.

But the most immediate advice to any company

thinking of buying gold is to discuss it with one of the leading bullion dealers. They are preparing specialized papers on the best utilization of gold by corporate buyers. And since the major American dealers all have close connections with traders in London and Zurich, they can draw on that European experience.

Corporate buyers should be interested primarily in gold bars of major value (i.e., 100-ounce and 400-ounce), because they bear a lower mark-up and have a lower trading spread. Alternatively, they will be able to buy central sealed bags or rolls of up to 1,000 Mexican, Austrian, or South African gold coins. Delivery will usually be in New York, Chicago, or Switzerland, and the gold can, of course, be stored in depositories there at fairly low charges.

Corporate buyers can also buy futures contracts, but the initial advice of some New York dealers was that a firm wishing to put $100,000 or more into gold might prefer to buy the actual metal, rather than deal in the speculative world of futures. Such gold would be left for safekeeping with the dealer, thus relieving the company of any worries of what actually to do with the stuff, and also eliminating the problem of assay being required when the gold is sold.

The eventual size of the investment market for gold in the U.S. will depend very much on corporate demand, for if even a modest number of companies switch only five percent or less of their assets into gold, then the annual offtake will run into several hundred tons. And that, in turn, will have considerable impact on the price.

If, as some advance surveys suggest, gold demand in the U.S., including corporate buying, goes as high as 600-800 tons a year, then (without central banks sales) the price would almost certainly go much higher. For 600 tons is about half of all the newly mined gold likely to reach the market in 1975. Corporate interest (or lack of it) in gold, therefore, can set the whole tone of the gold markets in the next year or two.

12 Gold Futures Markets

Anyone anxious to avoid the headaches of security, assaying, insurance, and storage of physical gold bars or coin may prefer to deal instead with the gold futures markets.

A futures market in gold has already been operating with considerable success in Winnipeg, Canada, since 1972. Several leading American bullion dealers and fabricators, licensed to trade in gold, have been using that market. But from December 31, 1974, at least four futures markets in gold will be operating in the United States. They are:

Gold Futures Markets

Exchange	Trading Unit	Fine-ness	Trading Hours	Minimum Fluct.	Daily Limit
Commodity Exchange Inc. (Comex) N.Y.	100 troy oz	995	10.15 A.M. 2.00 P.M.	5¢/0z	$ 8/0z
N.Y. Mercantile Exchange (Mercex)	1 kilo (32.15 oz)	995		5-10¢/0z	$10/0z
Chicago Board of Trade	3 one kilo bars (96.45 oz)	999.9	10.10 A.M. 2.10 P.M.	10¢/0z	$ 8/0z
International Monetary Market of Chicago Mercantile Exchange	100 troy oz	995	9.50 A.M. 2.10 P.M.	10¢/0z	$10/0z

The Mid-America and the Pacific Commodity Exchanges have also expressed their intention of trading in gold futures.

The futures market really appeals to two groups—hedgers and speculators.

The hedger uses the market principally as a marketing and price-protection mechanism for establishing the price at which he will buy or sell his inventory gold at a future day. Gold-mining companies, semi-fabricators, bullion dealers, and jewelery manufacturers all use the futures facilities. Good use of the market can stabilize income, provide flexibility in the timing of purchases and sales, reduce inventory costs, and free working capital. Gold-mining groups, for instance, can secure their income by selling production in advance, to protect themselves against a price decline.

The speculator, on the other hand, is in there for a gamble, to make money. He is using risk capital to gain from favorable price fluctuations by buying futures when he believes the price will go up, and selling when he feels it will go down. He is not normally concerned with handling the physical commodity; the speculator rarely takes delivery of his gold—he just sells his contract.

Market experts see the combination of the hedger and the speculator as vital to the successful functioning of a liquid futures market.

What exactly is a futures contract? And how does the market operate? Here's how the International Monetary Market of the Chicago Mercantile Exchange Inc. describes the set-up.

"A futures contract for gold is a legally-binding instrument to buy or sell a designated quantity of gold at a specified time period in the future, at a price agreed upon today." The time is usually three months, but may be longer. The price is actually arrived at by open, competitive bidding on the exchange floor by brokers accredited to the exchange. But, unlike the international gold price, there is a daily limit on how much the price can fluctuate: U.S. futures markets are selecting either $8 or $10 limits. That is to say, if the price is $180 today, it can go to $170 or $190 tomorrow. The precise size of the contract varies from exchange to exchange; the smallest contract announced is of 1 kilo at the New York Mercantile Exchange, but 100 ounces looks like the more popular contract elsewhere.

To confirm a contract, a buyer or seller is required to put up a deposit or margin, normally about 10% of the contract's value.

Once the contract has been purchased you can either sit on it and actually take delivery, or you simply liquidate it by selling.

Action in a gold futures market is not quite like a casino, but it can be risky. As the Chicago Mercantile Exchange warns potential speculators, "The gold futures market is not for the faint-hearted, nor should anything but *risk capital* be used for speculating in it, risk capital being money that could be lost without changing a person's way of life."

You have been warned. The gold futures markets are likely to appeal initially, apart from professional hedgers in mining or fabrication, to people with previous experience playing the other futures markets in everything from silver to soybeans. But if you do want to get some of the action, you should get all the detailed information published by the different exchanges (all listed in the Gold Buyer's Address Book), as precise regulations, size of contract, and size of margin will differ. These exchanges will also give you a complete list of all brokers approved to trade there on your behalf; and you will have to operate through one of these brokers.

Initial expectations are that the futures markets may become the focal point of most American gold buying. Since Americans have no tradition of buying bars of gold to hide under the bed and have no real reason to start now, the appeal of playing the futures markets may be paramount.

13 *Selling Your Gold*

Gold does not pay interest or dividends, so the key factor is to sell your gold at precisely the right moment and to ensure that when you do so you get the maximum profit.

Since the gold price has been highly volatile in the last three years, and can jump up—or down—by $20 or more in a week and even $10 in a day, you can make or lose money very quickly. Although you will see many charts and other special assessments of what the price will do, it is important to remember that nowadays gold is moving in uncharted waters. After being set at $35 an ounce for almost 40 years, it is now striving to seek its new natural level. If all the new gold was simply going into jewelery or industry it would be fairly easy to determine roughly how the price might move over the next year or two by balancing up supply and demand. But less than 50% of new gold now goes into jewelery or industry.

The main factor in the gold price today is investment buying by people worried about the economic and political future of their countries. Even the British, who have never been gold bugs, have suddenly become addicted to gold as a hedge against further devaluation of the £. And this investment demand can fluctuate wildly from day to day, depending on the advent of some new crisis.

So the question of when to sell is a tricky one. The price may coast along without much change for some weeks, and then jump $10 overnight due to some domestic crisis in France or rumors of a new Middle East outbreak.

The point is that the supply of new gold to the market daily is quite small—usually no more than 5 tons, worth between $25 million and $35 million, depending on the price. So any significant shift of investors' money into gold can do dramatic things to the price. Thirty-five million dollars, after all, is peanuts compared to the billions invested in Wall Street or accruing to the Arab oil nations.

In deciding whether or not to sell, you have to judge (or guess) just how much a particular crisis is going to affect the price and for how long.

The only general guide is this. If you have bought your gold at anything under $160 and the price goes over $200 an ounce, then it would be prudent to do at least some profit-taking. In fact, it may well prove a gamble to stay with gold at much over $200. Like all commodity prices, the gold price soars up and down in waves, and it is worth doing some profit-taking on the crests. That does not mean you dispose of all your holdings; you simply earn your dividend by selling part of your holding. And it is for this reason that the gold portfolios in tables 6-11 suggest holding a range of bars.

Although the trend of the gold price has been inexorably upward over the last few years, it could go down (though probably not under $130 to $140 for long). What about selling then? Here it depends if you are in for a long haul or just to make a quick profit. On the long haul, stay with it. If you are in gold for a quick turn, however, you will clearly give your bank or broker stop-loss orders to get rid of your gold at a certain level if the price starts to tumble. This at least minimizes your losses.

But if you are selling, either for a profit or stop-loss, keep in mind a few key technical points.

First, the spread on very small gold bars will be relatively wide—possibly as high as 4%. So if you are selling back 1-ounce or 5-ounce bars you will encounter quite a margin between bid and ask, which may not make the profit as great as you expected. On the other hand, the spread on large bars (100-ounce and 400-ounce) will be much narrower (probably less than 1%). On selling a large position in big bars you should get very close to the prevailing London price, less the dealer's handling charge. This should be as low as ¼% on major transactions, if the dealer is already holding the gold for you. In wholesale bullion trading in Europe, ¼% is considered a large mark-up.

On gold coins sold directly back to coin dealers in fairly small lots, you can usually expect a margin of about $3-$5 per coin between bid and ask on coins costing over $200, about $2 on coins in the range $100 to $200, and about $1.50 on coins under $100 each. As with buying, you should shop around several dealers before you sell; prices can vary by $2 to $3 per coin.

The second crucial fact to remember in selling your gold is that if you have taken delivery of bars they will only be bought back by a bank or bullion dealer subject to assay. This assay may cost as much as $75 to $150 per bar, and you will not get your money until it has been completed, which may be several days. This will apply even if you have only put the bars in your own safe deposit at the bank.

Therefore, as I have already suggested in earlier chapters, you should leave your gold with the bank or bullion dealer, in his custody. The bars can then be bought back immediately, without assay. True, the bank will have made a charge for storage and insurance, but this will have been fairly nominal and will almost certainly work out at less than having your money tied up for several days pending assay results.

You should find that repurchasing of bars you have left with a bank or dealer works very smoothly, because the leading refiners and bullion firms are anxious to establish a good two-way market in the United States. They have learnt this by seeing what happened in Japan when gold holding was liberalized there in 1973. In Japan, banks were not permitted to trade in gold, and no buy-back facilities were set up. So the Japanese rushed to buy gold, chiefly through department stores, but when the price went up found they could sell it back only to a very limited number of precious metal dealers, who offered them $5 or $10 below the market price. Leading American bullion firms have determined not to let this happen in the U.S., and organizations like Mocatta Metals Corporation and Engelhard have been setting up detailed repurchasing arrangements with banks and other wholesalers to whom they will be supplying gold.

So provided you do business with a first-class firm you should experience no difficulties. Let's hope you find it equally easy to sell at a profit.

Any profits you make from gold will be liable, of course, to federal income taxes, and you should also consult your tax counsel on your liability to state and local taxes on the profits of gold investments. Generally you should expect tax rules on the profits (and losses) of gold trading to be the same as on dealings in silver or other commodities.

14 The Gold Buyer's Address Book

BULLION AND COIN DEALERS (Wholesale)

U.S.A.

> J. Aron & Co., Inc.
> 160 Water Street
> New York, N.Y. 10038
> Phone: (212) 747-5300   Telex: (*domestic*) 125918

> Engelhard Minerals & Chemicals Corporation
> 430 Mountain Avenue
> Murray Hill, N.J. 07974
> Phone: (201) 464-7000   Telex: 13-8128

Engelhard Minerals & Chemicals Corporation
299 Park Avenue
New York, N.Y. 10017
Phone (212) PL2-4000

Federal Coin & Currency, Inc. (*Gold Coins Only*)
25 Broad Street
New York, New York 10004
Phone: (212) 785-1230 Telex: (domestic) 12-9262

Handy & Harman
850 Third Avenue
New York, N.Y. 10022
Phone: (212) 752-3400   Telex: 0126288

Mocatta Metals Corporation
25 Broad Street
New York, N.Y. 10004
Phone: (212) 785-1200   Telex: (*domestic*) 12-5053

Rhode Island Hospital Trust National Bank
One Hospital Trust Plaza
Providence, R.I. 02903. Phone: (401) 278-8676
Telex: 927619

Republic National Bank of New York
5th Avenue at 40th St.
New York, N.Y. 10018
Phone: (212) 524-9000   Telex 22-4967

Sharps Pixley, Inc.
100 Wall Street
New York, N.Y. 10005
Phone: (212) 248-5114

Canada

Bank of Nova Scotia
44 King St. W.
Toronto 1, Canada.
Phone: (416) 866-6161   Telex: 210-622106

Britain

Johnson Matthey (Bankers) Ltd.
15 King Street
London EC2

Samuel Montagu & Co. Ltd.
114 Old Broad Street
London EC2P 2HY
(*linked with Handy & Harman
and Merrill Lynch in U.S.*)

Mocatta & Goldsmid
16 Finsbury Circus
London EC2
(*associated with Mocatta
Metals Corporation in New York*)

N.M. Rothschild & Sons Ltd.
New Court
St. Swithins Lane
London EC4

Sharps Pixley & Co. Ltd.
20 Fenchurch St.
London EC3

Switzerland

Swiss Bank Corporation
Paradeplatz 6
8021 Zurich
Switzerland

Swiss Credit Bank
8 Paradeplatz
8021 Zurich
Switzerland

Union Bank of Switzerland
Bahnhofstrasse 45
8021 Zurich
Switzerland

FUTURES MARKETS

U.S.A.

Chicago Board of Trade
141 West Jackson Street
Chicago, Illinois
Phone: (312) 922-2800

International Monetary Market of
    Chicago Mercantile Exchange Inc.
444 West Jackson Boulevard
Chicago, Illinois 60606
Phone: (312) 648-1000

Commodity Exchange Inc. (*COMEX*)
81 Broad Street
New York, N.Y. 10004
Phone: (212) 943-5282

New York Mercantile Exchange
6 Harrison Street
New York, N.Y. 10013
Phone: (212) WO6-2600

Canada

The Winnipeg Commodity Exchange,
678-167 Lombard Avenue,
Winnipeg, Manitoba R3B OV7
Phone: (204) 942-6401

BANKS AND OTHER RETAIL OUTLETS
*(This list includes only those institutions that had announced
their intention to sell gold at the time of going to press.)*

California

Wells Fargo Bank
464 California St.
San Francisco, Cal. 49104

Illinois

The First National Bank of Chicago
One First National Plaza
Chicago, Ill. 60670

New York

First National City Bank of New York
399 Park Avenue
New York, N.Y. 10022

Republic National Bank of New York
5th Avenue at 40th St.
New York, N.Y. 10018
And at 17 branches in New York area

Terminal Trading Co.
61 W. 23rd St.
New York, N.Y. 10011
And at New York branches

Pennsylvania

Girard Trust Bank
3 Girard Plaza
Philadelphia, Penn. 19101

Tennessee

First American National Bank of Nashville
326 Union Street
Nashville, Tenn. 37202

Virginia

Bank of Virginia Co.
800 East Main Street
Richmond, Virginia 23214

BROKERAGE FIRMS WITH
SPECIAL INTEREST IN GOLD

Bache & Co., Inc.
100 Gold Street
New York, N.Y. 10038

Drexel Burnham & Co., Inc.
60 Broad St.
New York, N.Y. 10004

Merrill Lynch, Pierce, Fenner & Smith Inc.
1 Liberty Plaza
165 Broadway
New York, N.Y. 10006
And offices across the U.S.A.

GOLD FUNDS

Bars of Gold, Inc.
One Wall Street
New York, N.Y. 10005

NORTH AMERICAN COIN DEALERS

Arizona

Lee's Stamp & Coin Shop
218 North First Street
Phoenix, Ariz. 85004

California

American Coin Company
6354 Van Nuys Blvd.
Van Nuys, Cal. 91401

Camino Coin
5 West 37th Ave.
San Mateo, Cal. 94403

H. & S. Gordon, Numismatics
9401 Wilshire Boulevard
Beverly Hills, Cal. 90210

Robert R. Johnson Inc.
353 Geary St.
San Francisco, Calif. 94102

S.J. Kabealo
2216 East Colorado Blvd.
Pasadena, Cal. 91107

Samuel M. Keoppel
307 West 8th St.
Los Angeles, Cal. 90014

A. Kosoff
P.O. Box 456
Encino, Cal. 91316

Abner Kreisberg
228 North Beverly Drive
Beverly Hills, Cal. 90210

E.A. Parker
1254 Market Street
San Francisco, Cal. 94102

Superior Stamp & Coin Co.
517 West 7th Street
Los Angeles, Calif. 90014

Colorado

Overton Coin Co.
336 Colorado Building
Pueblo, Colo. 81001

Connecticut

Cohn Precious Metals Inc.
39 Church Street
New Haven, Conn. 06502

District of Columbia

Frank J. Katen
1444 Primrose Road N.W.
Washington, D.C. 20012

The Henry Co.
1028-1032 Investment Building
Washington, D.C. 20005

Woodward & Lothrop
Rare Coin Dept.
10th and F Streets N.W.
Washington, D.C. 20001

Florida

Italcambio
P.O. Box 61-1358
1470 N.E. 129th St.
N. Miami, Fla. 33161

Miami Rare Coin Co.
2045 Biscayne Boulevard
Miami, Fla. 33137

James P. Randall
P.O. Box 2205
Coolee Station
Fort Lauderdale, Fla. 33303

Georgia

Rich's Department Store
Coin Dept.
45 Broad Street S.W.
Atlanta, Ga. 30303

Illinois

Ben's Stamp & Coin Co.
31 North Clark Street
Chicago, Ill. 60602

First National Bank of Chicago
One First National Plaza
Chicago, Ill. 60670

Marshall Field & Co.
Rare Coin Dept.
111 North State Street
Chicago, Ill. 60602

Rare Coin of Chicago
31 N. Clarke Street
Chicago, Ill. 60602

Indiana

Nunemaker's
105 Hope Blvd.
Bremen, Ind. 46506

Engle's Coin Shop
6020 E. 82 Dr. East
P.O. Box 500951
Indianapolis, Ind. 46250

Silver Towne
P.O. Box 424
Winchester, Ind. 47394

Iowa

Lauren Benson
P.O. Box 871
Davenport, Iowa 52808

Hollinbeck Kagin Coin Co.
Suite 400-03
Royal Union Building
Des Moines, Iowa 52809

Kansas

Joe Flynn, Sr., Coin Co.
2854 W. 47th Street
Box 3140
Kansas City, Kansas 66103

Sunflower Coins
537 Marceline Terrace
Wichita, Kan. 67218

Kentucky

James, Inc.
105 West Main Street
Louisville, Ky. 40202

Lee's Coin Shop
P.O. Box 58
Hardin, Ky. 42048

Louisiana

Orleans Coin Shop
517 Baronne Street
New Orleans, La. 70113

Maine

Wm. H. Kenworthy
44 Main Stret
Waterville, Maine 04901

Maryland

Alfred Hutter
P.O. Box 122
Cumberland, Md. 21502

Mason-Dixon Coin Exchange
208 West Saratoga Street
Baltimore, Md. 21201

Massachusetts

Boston Towne Coin Exchange
120 Tremont Street
Boston, Mass. 02108

Ambrose J. Brown
63 Pond Street
Marblehead, Mass. 01945

Copley Coin Company
581 Boylston Street
Boston, Mass. 02116

Court Coin Company
33 Court Street
Boston, Mass. 02108

Mayflower Coin Auctions Inc.
53 Bromfield Street
Boston, Mass. 02108

Cash Coin Exchange Center Inc.
40 Court Street
Government Center
Boston, Mass. 02108

Michigan

Coin Investments, Inc.
725 S. Adams
Birmingham, Mich. 48011

Detroit Coin Co.
818 Lawrence Avenue
Detroit, Mich. 48202

J.L. Hudson Co.
Rare Coin Department
1206 Woodward Street
Detroit, Mich. 48226

Earl Schill
110 John R Street
Detroit, Mich. 48226

Minnesota

Ruber Stamp & Coin Co.
210 South 6th Street
Minneapolis, Minn. 55402

Sullivan Stamp & Coin Co.
127 East 4th Street
St. Paul, Minn. 55101

Missouri

Hansan's Coin Shop
1404 Main Street
Kansas City, Mo. 64105

Joplin Coin Shop
813 Main Street
Joplin, Mo. 64801

Art Kelley
4314 Olive Street
St. Louis, Mo. 63108

Nebraska

Bebee's
4514 North 30th St.
Omaha, Neb.

Nevada

Imperial Coin Co.
P.O. Box 189
Las Vegas, Nev. 89101

New Jersey

Garden State Coin Exchange
69 Main Street
Hackensack, N.J. 07601

Numismatic Co. of America
P.O. Box 711
Springfield, N.J. 07081

New York

Joel D. Coen, Inc.
39 West 55th Street
New York, N.Y. 10019

Henry Christensen
545 Fifth Avenue
New York, N.Y. 10017

Federal Coin & Currency, Inc.
25 Broad Street
New York, New York 10004

Empire Coin Company Inc.
252 Main Street
Johnson City, N.Y. 13790

First Coinvestors, Inc.
200 I. U. Willets
Albertson, N.Y. 11507

French's
7 First Street
Troy, N.Y. 12180

Robert Friedberg
134 West 32nd Street
New York, N.Y. 10001

Gimbel's
33rd & Broadway
New York, N.Y. 10001

Max Hirschhorn
34-08 Northern Boulevard
Long Island City, N.Y. 11101

M.L. Kaplan
550 Fifth Avenue
New York, N.Y. 10017

Manfra, Tordella & Brookes
59 West 49th Street
New York, N.Y. 10020

New Netherlands Coin Co., Inc.
1 West 47th Street
New York, N.Y. 10036

Saturn Stamp Company
754 Main Street
Buffalo, N.Y. 14202

Hans M.F. Schulman
545 Fifth Avenue
New York, N.Y. 10017

Stack's
123 West 57th Street
New York, N.Y. 10019

Syracuse Stamp & Coin Co.
217 East Fayette Street
Syracuse, N.Y. 13202

Wall Street Precious Metals Exchange
2 West 45th Street
New York, N.Y. 10036

Louis S. Werner
1270 Broadway
New York, N.Y. 10001

Ohio

Federal Coin Exchange
5940 Pearl Road
Cleveland, O. 44130

Sol Kaplan
413 Race Street
Cincinnati, O. 45202

James Kelley
World Numismatiques, Inc.
333 West First Street
Dayton, O. 45402

Riggs Coin Co.
525 Walnut Street
Cincinnati, O. 45216

Oregon

The Coin Shop
423 SW Washington Street
Portland, Ore. 97204

Columbia Coin Co.
407 S.W. Washington
Portland, Ore. 97204

Pennsylvania

David M. Bullowa
37 South 18th Street
Philadelphia, Pa. 19103

Pittsburgh Coin Exchange
707 Park Building
Pittsburgh, Pa. 15222

Rhode Island

Horace M. Grant
109 Empire Street
Providence, R.I. 02903

Tennessee

Chattanooga Coin Co., Inc.
P.O. Box 1028-CW
Chattanooga, Tenn. 37401

Texas

El Paso Coin Co., Inc.
P.O. Box Q.
El Paso, Tex. 79952

Colonial Coin Co.
909 Travis
P.O. Box 19372
Houston, Texas 77002

Rare Coin, Inc.
2001 Bryan Tower, #2205
Dallas, Texas 75201

Security National Rare Coin Corp.
429 E. Commerce, Suite 4
San Antonio, Texas 78205

Utah

Norman Shultz
P.O. Box 746
Salt Lake City, Utah 84110

Virginia

Washington Coin Exchange
5205 Leesburg Pike, Suite 310
Bailey's Crossroads, Va. 22041

Washington

Paul Fouts
609 People's Building
Seattle, Wash.

Wisconsin

Gimbel's
Rare Coin Department
101 West Wisconsin Avenue
Milwaukee, Wis. 53203

ADDENDUM

As of January 6, 1975, the following information pertaining to sales taxes was in
effect:

Forty-five of the fifty states (all but
Alaska, Delaware, Montana, New Hampshire and
Oregon) impose a tax on the retail sale of
tangible personal property within the state.
These sales taxes must be paid by the buyer
of the property, but the seller has the ob-
ligation to collect the tax and remit it to

the appropriate revenue authorities. Gold, whether in the form of coin or bullion, is considered tangible personal property and therefore is subject to sales taxes. California is the only state whose sales tax currently exempts some forms of precious metals-- "monetized bullion" having a U.S. currency face value equivalent of $1000 or more -- but this exemption was designed for sales of U.S. silver coins as a commodity and may not be applicable to gold coins. A purchase of 50 Double Eagles would be the minimum exempt quantity, for example. Other states are understood to have similar exemptions or special rates for gold under consideration.

Since sales tax rates range as high as 8%, it is obvious that the applicability of the tax to gold -- which is normally purchased for investment purposes -- puts gold at a severe disadvantage compared to competing investment media such as stocks, bonds and certificates of deposit, which involve either no tax or a tax of de minimus magnitude. Thus, the need to structure gold investments to avoid sales tax has been perhaps the most significant factor in determining the storage locations of gold which Americans are offered.

This odd state of affairs derives from the fact that, as stated, the tax applies only to sales "within " a taxing state, and some unexpected doctrine has developed on where a sale takes place. In general, the sale is considered to occur in the jurisdiction in which title changes hands. This, in turn, is thought to occur in the jurisdiction where the physical object is located at the time title passes. Therefore, if the gold is held in storage in a sales tax-free jurisdiction when the buyer purchases, there is no sale of tangible property in either the seller's or the buyer's state even if both are sales tax jurisdictions. This result is believed to occur whether the material is stored in a state without a sales tax, such as Delaware, or a foreign country. The popularity of gold purchase programs involving transfer of title to material stored in Delaware or Switzerland (such as Mocatta Metals Delivery Orders and National-Unit-Gold-Trust) results from the opportunity they provide for avoiding sales taxes in a completely legal manner.

The gold buyer who purchases gold stored in a tax-free jurisdiction should be aware that, if he later arranges for shipment of the gold to his home state, he might have to pay a "compensating use" tax, the amount of which will equal the sales tax. There is of course no sales or use tax due if he sells the gold without it ever having entered his state.